THE PASSION

And

PURPOSE PROJECT

Cheers!
Kiry ♡

THE PASSION

And

PURPOSE PROJECT

---

*Your 7-Step Future Funnel to Design
the Life You Were Meant to Live*

By

KIMMY K. POWELL

THE PASSION AND PURPOSE PROJECT
Your 7-Step Future Funnel to Design the Life You Were Meant to Live

POWELL, KIMMY K., Author
THE PASSION AND PURPOSE PROJECT
KIMMY K. POWELL

Published by:
ELITE ONLINE PUBLISHING
63 East 11400 South
Suite #230
Sandy, UT 84070
EliteOnlinePublishing.com

ISBN: 978-1-956642-60-5 (Paperback)
ISBN: 978-1-956642-59-9 (eBook)

BUS046000
SEL027000

Edited by Tim Mitchell

QUANTITY PURCHASES: Schools, companies, professional groups, clubs, and other organizations may qualify for special terms when ordering quantities of this title. For information, email info@ eliteonlinepublishing.com.

DEDICATION

*T*his book is dedicated to my mother, the unlikeliest of entrepreneurs. She always said to me, "I never really discovered my purpose." It's hard for me to reconcile how I feel about that. On the one hand, if she wouldn't have dedicated her entire heart and soul to her family, I'm fairly certain none of us would have become who we are today. She instilled love, joy, confidence, courage, hope, exuberance, kindness, compassion, and so much more by loving us unconditionally. On the other hand, her love for the piano, sewing, and countless unidentified joys may have gone untapped in the process.

Technically, she's not considered an entrepreneur, but the fact that she filled me with confidence and curiosity is a commodity that I simply couldn't have purchased anywhere else.

So, I dedicate this with the hope that as she approaches the swan song of her life, knowing that while she felt she was eluding her true purpose, she was actually living it.

Thank you Momma (AKA Gangsta Grandma)!

"Life doesn't come with a manual, it comes with a mother."

— Unknown

ACKNOWLEDGEMENTS

I would like to acknowledge those who encouraged me to write this book and cheered me on along the way. I decided to write this book because I am often asked for advice about entrepreneurship, career aspirations, solving a business problem, etc. I can only draw from three decades of failures and successes, but in the end, I've found that it really always boils down to the 3 P's: Passion, Purpose, and Perseverance.

Buckley, Bowen, and Christian, my three sons, inspired me by their countless teenage shenanigans to escape into the world of entrepreneurship and show them firsthand what they did not seem to be learning in school. I'm very grateful for their inspiration because it truly gave me the fuel that I needed to move to a new city and start a new career. It's funny that what you won't or are too embarrassed to do for yourself, is often the thing that you need to do and somehow doing it for someone else is just less scary. My boys have grown into very responsible and entrepreneurial adults, and I am glad that we continue to have great conversations about work, investments, family, and entrepreneurship.

And last, but certainly not least, my husband, Keith, who was an entrepreneur from birth, has especially given me inspiration. Having to rely only on himself, he managed to create an exceptional life that I have loved sharing with him. Here's the thing about entrepreneurs, you don't have to be Warren Buffett, Sara Blakely, or Elon Musk. You simply have to be you. Unapologetically, you! There is no prize, scale, or score card. Money certainly is not a measure of success as an entrepreneur in my book (it's literally my book so I can say that not just metaphorically). To me, the real measure of an entrepreneur is being authentic. It's your passion, it's your purpose. You need to be brave enough to be you. Keith exudes that for me! No, he doesn't have a filter, so that's at times cringe worthy, but he's real. Let's be real!

TABLE OF CONTENTS

Introduction

But First...How Does This Story End?

"How we spend our days is, of course, how we spend our lives."

— Annie Dillard

*T*he quotation above from Annie Dillard is simple common sense yet thought provoking at that same time. The poignant message behind this short sentence is to make sure what you do each day focuses on the type of life you really want. How does that translate into your life? Well, simply in this manner. It's very likely that you are working daily to receive income so you can achieve what you really want in life. However, it is quite easy to get caught up in income producing activity and miss what you really want in life. Are you going to live the life of your dreams or are you going to be a slave to the mundane?

So, how do you live the life of your dreams? I believe the answer to that question lies in another very important question, "Am I putting my outcome before my income?" Do you know very specifically what you want as your life outcome? If not, that is where you need to begin. Life has a way of interfering with the best laid plans. But, if you are starting out without any direction, the circumstances you encounter throughout your lifetime will surely hinder you from actually achieving anything significant.

Most people get hung up on this issue right out of the gate. How many high school graduates do you know who have their life's plan specifically mapped out? For that matter, how many middle-aged people do you know who have such a precise plan in place? Unfortunately, this is a step most people miss in their career planning. Instead of considering their desired outcome, they pick up a job that pays them the most money at the time. Often this job is something they grow to despise, or at least not like, but it pays the bills. So, they go to work, day after day, grumbling and complaining, so they can live week after week. Most Americans do not enjoy their work. They just work for a paycheck.

It's never too late to consider your outcome before your income and there is no better time to start than now. You may be wondering, "How do I consider my outcome before my income?" and "Exactly what does that even mean?"

Considering your outcome before your income simply means exploring life in reverse and then backing into the life you were meant to live by design. This is something I like to call YOUR FUTURE FUNNEL™. The diagram below illustrates the various levels of the funnel, and we will consider each aspect throughout this book.

You may be a young person just now starting to determine your career possibilities or you may

YOUR FUTURE FUNNEL™

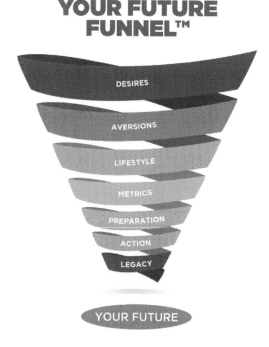

DESIRES

AVERSIONS

LIFESTYLE

METRICS

PREPARATION

ACTION

LEGACY

YOUR FUTURE

be an individual who has 20 or 30 or more years of work experience behind you, but it doesn't feel like you are doing what you should be doing with your life. Whatever stage of life you are in, as you consider your future, ask yourself this question, "What is the purpose of my life's work?" and "What should be the purpose of my life's work?" Digging deep into what you truly want to achieve is a critical first step.

Remember, the goal is to take a deep dive into Your Future Funnel™. It's very common to have the tendency to float back to the top of the funnel because you're afraid of drowning. But treading water at the top of the funnel is exhausting. If you stay there for an extended length of time you will likely drown in the waters of the mundane and never fulfill your dreams or live the lifestyle you desire. Realistically, going through the steps of this funnel may sometimes feel overwhelming and you may feel like you are drowning emotionally. However, the only way to make it through is to swim toward your desired future. *So don't float back to the top of the funnel!*

We all wrestle with questions at different times in our life. We all have dreams and aspirations that may seem unattainable. But are they really outside our reach or have we just convinced ourselves that it will never happen? As I have worked with and coached many people over the years, the recurring questions I hear on this subject are the following: "I have so many passions, where do I start?" "What if I don't know what I want to do?" "How do I find a way to live a different lifestyle?" This book will help you answer those burning questions.

Why Passion + Purpose + Project? Three seemingly unrelated and simple words, but their meaning will create the most incredible life, yours! We plan vacations, design homes, decorate for parties, and host incredible culinary events, but we spend so little time designing our lives.

Well, NO MORE! If you're reading this page your life is about to change! Be prepared to have a lot of fun, feel alive, and connected!

As you will discover, I always wanted to be a teacher, so this is my big break. In this book,

I want to teach you by assigning you a project to complete.

Assignment: Find your passion and purpose.

Instructions: Bring a notebook with you because you will create a working document outlining the steps YOU need to take in order to live with passion, purpose, and authenticity. You are to allow yourself to dream without imaginary boundaries.

Grading: You will be graded on the happiness you fill yourself with and the joy you share with others.

Due Date: Whenever you want your assignment to be completed. It's entirely up to you. Take your time but stay focused.

Harriet Tubman said, *"Every great dream begins with a dreamer. Always remember, you have within you the strength, the patience, and the passion to reach for the stars to change the world."*

Let's do this!

YOUR FUTURE
FUNNEL™

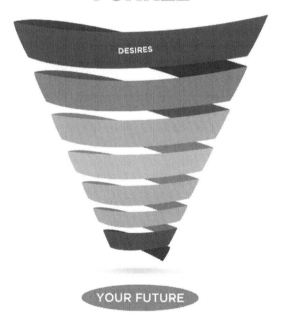

DESIRES

YOUR FUTURE

Chapter 1

It Resides Within...You Just Have to Awaken Your Inner Child
Level 1 – Desires

"The question should be who do we want to be when we grow up, not what."

— Craig Stone

Question: I have so many passions, where do I start?

*I*n order to get to your real passion in life, you must uncover your underlying "desires," that may have been dormant for years. Napoleon Hill so fittingly said, "The starting point of all achievement is desire. Keep this constantly in mind. Weak desires bring weak results, just like a small amount of fire makes a small amount of heat."

What are your desires? Sometimes it's challenging to uncover your real desires and passions because they seem to get buried under the giant snowball of life events. I tell those that I mentor, "You start with your inner child, where it all began." What did you want to be when you were growing up? What was your earliest passion that you can remember as a kid? When you were all alone in your room as a child, what did you most like to do? These desires are often very telling.

Unfortunately, as we grow older, we grow out of our inner child, and that's too bad.

Because your inner child knows what they want to do. It's the adult that messes up the inner child and we spend a lot of our adult life trying to get back to being a kid again and doing what we always loved to do as a child.

Personally, I grew up wanting to be a teacher. I distinctly remember going to my elementary school on a teacher in-service day and got all the teacher editions of the books so I could have all the answers. Then after school, I would pretend to teach a class. I truly had a passion for teaching! So, if I look back on that time in my young life, I can see that I obviously wanted to teach, that I liked people, and that I wanted to help them. It is interesting that when you think of a teacher, your mind automatically pictures a schoolteacher. But I didn't need to be a schoolteacher to foster my love of teaching.

It is very important that you don't pigeonhole your passion. Once I realized I could incorporate teaching into many parts of my life, I felt more fulfilled and confident. I discovered I can teach people about wellness by having a wellness spa.

Now, I can see how that passion can also be used in many other ways, like becoming a business owner, expanding into the hospitality industry, becoming a public speaker and author, or a myriad of other avenues I can pursue in order to fulfill my passion to teach and help others.

I now do a lot of mentoring, which I love. I'm on the Board of Governors for the College of Charleston, and mentor there occasionally. I have over 100 employees who are like students to me, and I enjoy seeing their successes and helping them along through their journey. So, even though I didn't turn out to be a schoolteacher, I ended up in a business that uses those God given talents and interests in a way that is fulfilling to me. It's very exciting, sort of like the first day of school. It never feels like work to me, that's how I know it's true passion. So, take some time to go back to your inner child.

If you aren't resonating with the inner child concept, then think about what you do on the weekends. What do you do when you're home alone? What brings you joy and what is your natural interest? Do you enjoy spending your time outside or inside? Some of those basic questions will help you to begin to identify with your desires and your God given talents. So, take a little time to remember who you were, who you wanted to be, and who that inner person is that brings you joy.

The end goal of your original passion may change, but you will discover that the same drive and set of values instilled in you by that passion can be the source of many choices. That is why it's so important to go back to your inner child. Don't forget about what you have wanted to do your entire life.

When I was in my teen-years I landed my first job. I actually lied about my age to get that first position as a Candy Striper at a hospital. For those too young to know the term "Candy Striper," we were young ladies who assisted patients in the hospital in various, non-medical, ways. The term "Candy Striper" is derived from the red-and-white striped pinafores that the volunteers traditionally wore which were reminiscent of candy canes. It was a volunteer position, so I made no money at all. But I loved it! I loved talking to people. I served from the beverage cart on the fifth floor of the hospital, and I was able to develop relationships with the patients. If I apply the inner child concept here, it makes sense that I've ended up in hospitality and in the service of others.

I discovered throughout the course of my life that not only do I like being around people, but I also like caring for them. Some part of me must have known from a very young age that I need to be around people. I like to see people succeed. I want to help them feel good and become their best in any way I can, whether it's through acts of service or just encouraging words.

I was also a cheerleader from seventh through twelfth grade and at one time served as the captain of the squad. I have always loved cheering people on. I enjoyed cheering for our athletic teams and supporting our community.

It's no surprise that today I own multiple spas with many therapists, mentor or "cheer on" students at The College of Charleston, and donate to various charities in my community. If you genuinely take a few minutes to consider your inner child, character traits will begin to emerge that will become the foundation of this new life you're designing.

Allow me now to fast forward to the life I came to live, but it wasn't really the life I wanted. I lived in Dayton, Ohio my entire life before moving to where I desired to live. After living in Dayton for nearly 45 years, I grew to have a great passion to live somewhere near water, in a warmer climate, and in a bigger city. Not only was location important, but I also knew that I needed to make a change in my career.

Quite frankly, at that point I wasn't really sure what I wanted to do. So, I can totally relate to anybody reading this book who knows you want to change something but aren't really sure how to change or what to change about your life. I was very intimidated and overwhelmed at the thought of making such big changes, but I knew I needed to do it. I came to a place I refer to as my "tipping point," a term you will see multiple times as you progress through the chapters that follow."

At the time, my husband and I had a nearly 25-year-old business, my mother, father, sister, cousins, and three children to consider as well as all of our employees. Everything, my entire life, was in Dayton! The thought of leaving was so overwhelming I didn't even really know where to start. It was almost stagnating! Remember, you will also likely feel the overwhelming pressure of change that may scare you, but you must not allow your dream to succumb to your fear!

My husband is originally from South Carolina and while raising our children we often traveled to the Beaufort, Fripp Island, and Hilton Head Island area which was always our home away from home. We were certain that we wanted to retire in that vicinity and had already taken steps to buy property to retire on a little island called Dataw Island. So, we had what we thought was at least a rough plan.

After our oldest son, Buckley, went to college at the University of South Carolina, and then transferred to the College of Charleston, to swim, we began to think more and more about moving to South Carolina. That was about the time our middle son was nearing his senior year in high school.

As fate would have it, I went to see my oldest son swim at the College of Charleston. Although we built a home on Fripp Island, just outside of Beaufort, had worked on Hilton Head Island and bought a home on Dataw Island, somehow, I had never been to Charleston!

I was blown away by this beautiful city. It was absolutely love at first sight for me! Immediately I knew this is where I would die. I know that sounds a little morbid and crazy, but that's exactly how I felt. At that point, I was so inspired and motivated, nothing was going to stop me. The desire I had been searching for had been birthed in me at that very moment. I was so inspired I was determined to find a way to live in Charleston. This is a good reminder that inspiration lies everywhere if you're open to finding it. It also illustrates the "outcome before income" mindset. I now had a "passion" and an "outcome" to work towards. It doesn't have to be so hard to find a new path, just look for what brings you joy.

Our middle son, Bowen, then began to explore options of going to college in the South, as well as in the Midwest. And, as luck would have it, he also ended up getting accepted to the College of Charleston. At that point we had two of our three children heading to Charleston or already in Charleston. So, like any good parents, we persuaded our youngest son, Christian, who was just finishing eighth grade, to come along with us (thank you Chris!). The thought of starting in a new city near his brothers and near water was exciting for him and exciting for us as well. With everyone on board, we all made the permanent move down to Charleston in June of 2014. Change is a powerful thing and I'm starting to believe more and more that we need to do it more often. Shake things up, chart a new course, make a new adventure for ourselves.

Prior to relocating, I often dreamt about life in Charleston. As a big fan of the Woodhouse Spa in Dayton, Ohio, I was hoping there would be one in Charleston since it was a franchise. I had grown accustomed to escaping to the Woodhouse Spa from time to time and hoped to continue that luxury in our new community. After some investigation and to my chagrin, I discovered there were no Woodhouse Spas in the entire southeast, let alone, South Carolina, or Charleston.

At that point, I began to explore the idea of opening a Woodhouse Spa franchise in Charleston. So, while still living in Dayton, I took my husband to brunch and to the Woodhouse Spa for massages one afternoon.

It worked! He was intrigued and agreed to fly down to Texas to learn more about owning a franchise. The CEO of Woodhouse Spas will tell you we were the fastest franchisees in their history to visit them and make a commitment to become a franchisee. As I look back on that time, I think I made such a quick decision because sometimes you're so scared you make decisions before you can talk yourself out of it.

Interestingly, about six months prior to that I had actually floated the franchisee idea to a friend of mine who was in the massage business and owns a massage school. That friend sort of talked me out of it by saying, "Why wouldn't you just open your own? Why do you need to do a franchise?" Those were definitely valid points to take under consideration. However, when you're trying to make a change it's easy to fall into listening to the naysayers because they validate your fears, and it becomes an easy out for you. You concede, "I thought about it, I talked to somebody about it, and it's not a good idea." But I caution anyone to not take the easy way out. If you do, you will likely not fulfill your true desires. It takes a considerable amount of effort and bravery to move into something entirely new.

Six months later I revisited the idea and made a commitment before I talked myself out of it again. So, before we moved to Charleston, I had already committed to opening the first Woodhouse Spa in the South and had begun looking at properties to house the Spa. Shortly after moving to Charleston, I found the property, bought it, and began the journey of spa ownership.

As I look back, the life I'm living now began simply by identifying that I wanted to live in the South and falling in love with the city of Charleston. Your journey may be different. You might be happy in the city in which you live, which in turn will save you a lot of time. Or you might also be interested in relocating and that's exciting too. At the end of the day, this book is called, Passion and Purpose, because you want to have passion and a purpose for where you live. If you don't live somewhere that you are passionate about, that makes finding your desire more difficult.

So, I would ask that you write down your desires and think long and hard about where you live. Are you genuinely happy there and does it feed your passions? Even if you stay within the same state or city, are you living in the right community or neighborhood you really desire? Where you live is a big factor in how you live. You spend a lot of time in your home, so it should be a space that makes you happy and brings you joy.

Originally, when we moved to South Carolina, we lived in a beautiful home at a marina. I thought I was the luckiest woman in the entire world. I couldn't believe that I had a palm tree outside my window and lived so close to our boat! It was everything for which I could have ever dreamed. But unfortunately, in a short amount of time, my husband and I realized that we weren't happy there. It took us another two years before we relocated to downtown Charleston where we live now. And, it would take us another two years to identify and buy our "forever home" which I will tell you more about in the Happy Endings chapter. The point is to love where you live and know that you can live anywhere you desire.

It's important that you know all your desires. It's not just the job you want or the right home. It's everything. It's the climate, the community, the job, and the people who are near you. It's the whole package. So, take your time and know that not everything can be changed overnight. But you can begin to plant the seeds, make the lists, daydream, and build your dreams and desires.

Remember, your innermost desires are often rooted in your childhood. What do you remember from your childhood? I encourage you to make a list of things you have enjoyed doing in your childhood and teenage years and the personality traits that accompanied those passions. For example, one of the things I mentioned is I enjoyed being a Candy Striper. The personality traits that it took to do that job included being caring, compassionate and enjoying serving others. You may find this brief exercise to be quite enlightening and it may help you discover your true passion in life. You may want to ask a friend or family member to help you identify things that may not be immediately clear to you.

Here is an exercise to work through. Below is a simple matrix that I have found helpful when trying to uncover my true desires and potential work. I have used myself as an example, filling in the matrix as it applies to me. Try this alone or possibly with a family member or friend. Start by writing down the "Things You Enjoy Doing" and then the associated "Desired Traits." This simple exercise may help move you toward a decision about your work life. Here is my example:

KIMMY

Things You Enjoy Doing	Desired Traits
Volunteering at a hospital	Serving others
Captain of cheerleading squad	Leadership/Mentoring
Playing Teacher	Teaching/Coaching
Love going to spas	Health/Wellness/Travel

YOUR FUTURE FUNNEL™

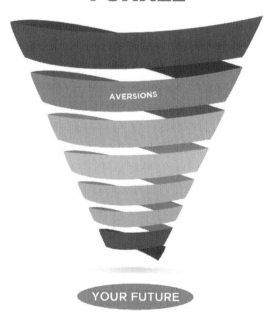

AVERSIONS

YOUR FUTURE

Chapter 2

Ruling Out the Obvious…
You Know What You
Don't Want
Level 2 - Aversions

"Knowing what you don't want to do is the best possible place to be if you don't know what to do. Because knowing what you don't want to do leads you to figure out what it is you really do want to do."

— Oprah Winfrey

Question: What if I don't know what I want to do?

*L*et me begin responding to this question by assuring you that it's perfectly okay to not know what you want to do in life. I was there too. I had so many differing passions and interests, but just didn't know how to develop them into a career or life plan. We've all heard the expression I referenced in the previous chapter, "tipping point." That's exactly what has to happen. A "tipping point" happens when the thought of staying the same is scarier than the idea of changing and we all need to experience that decisive moment if we are going to advance in life.

For example, I knew I wanted to move to Charleston, South Carolina. I knew I needed to be by the water. I knew that I owned a business in Ohio with my husband that did not feed my soul. And, I knew it would mean leaving my lifelong friends and family.

However, I came to a "tipping point" in my life when I came to the realization that the idea of staying the same was more frightening than the idea of changing. I like to call this the "treadmill syndrome." That is, you go through days, weeks, months, and years of your life doing the same thing over and over and never really getting where you want to be. It's like being on a treadmill - you do a lot of walking, but you get nowhere. I was finally ready and willing to focus on moving, creating a plan, and taking the leap of faith. You have to be willing to take the leap, but once you set your mind to it, the universe finds a way to catch you in mid-air and get you safely to the other side.

A good place to start is to make a list of things you absolutely *DON'T* want to do. It helps to get those items off the drawing board so you can begin focusing on the things for which you are passionate. This is the second stage of YOUR FUTURE FUNNEL™, AVERSIONS. A mentor can be very beneficial in this regard. Sometimes it helps to say out loud to another person what you're thinking, and an experienced mentor, business coach, or life coach will know what questions to ask you to help you uncover the things you are certain you don't want to do and lead you toward your proposed objective.

Aversions are obviously things that you absolutely know you don't want to do. As I mentioned previously, I knew I absolutely didn't want to live in the Midwest anymore! I could not take any more of the gray cloudy days and the snow and ice was just too much for me. I also knew that continuing to work with my husband and our construction company wasn't fulfilling me. I loved the business, but it wasn't the right business "fit" for me. It did not resonate with me or my true passion, interests, and talents. I felt those things were being wasted and stifled. I also realized I was close to becoming an empty nester and I wanted something that I could do for the rest of my life. I wanted a business that I could do on my own and was something I really enjoyed. That's how I ended up focusing on Woodhouse Spas.

It's important to think about *where* you *don't* want to live and *how* you *don't* want to live, and ask yourself these questions: In what states and cities do I *not* want to live? In what climate do I *not* want to live? In what kind of house do I *not* want to live? What kind of job do I *not* want? You may not know exactly what you do want yet, but you really need to be thinking about what you know you don't want anymore. Chances are, you already have a running list in your mind from experience. It all starts with a list.

Eliminating what I knew I didn't want to do and focusing on those innate characteristics that defined me as a person since childhood was a real paradigm shift for me. It was then that I began to shift my focus and look for opportunities that I would love. The key here is the shift.

Paula Deen, an American television personality and cooking show host, is a great example to consider. Unfortunately, her parents died before she was 23, and her early marriage ended in divorce. These traumatic events no doubt contributed to the onset of her bouts with panic attacks and agoraphobia, a type of anxiety disorder in which you fear and avoid places or situations that might cause you to panic and make you feel trapped, helpless, or embarrassed.

To compensate for this condition, she focused on cooking for her family as something she could do without leaving her house. During her childhood, Paula's grandmother taught her the hand-me-down art of Southern cooking. One of the only places she felt safe was at her own stove, making thousands of pots of chicken and dumplings.

She later moved to Savannah, Georgia, with her sons. In 1989, she divorced her husband, Jimmy Deen, to whom she had been married since 1965. She was left with only $200, and money was tight raising both her kids and her younger brother. She tried hanging wallpaper, working as a bank teller, and selling real estate and insurance. Only to discover, those were things she did not want to do and for which she had no passion. She then returned to her cooking roots and started a catering service out of her home called The Bag Lady, making sandwiches and meals, which her sons delivered.

This was the beginning of Paula Deen's breakthrough. After discovering what she didn't want to do, she still had no clue about what she did want to do with her life. Then she began looking at what she did well. She evaluated her skill set, "What do I do well?" "What do I know best?" "What am I passionate about?" Now, answering those questions didn't automatically put her in front of the cameras. But it did lead her to start out as a sandwich designer. That may sound quite random, but it caught the attention of the right people and turned into a successful business. It was a business idea, driven by her passion to be in the kitchen creating delicious meals.

Stop here and just think about this for a few minutes. We sometimes refer to this as "inspiration or desperation." It's that time when you are either inspired to do something or desperate to get out of an unfulfilling situation. In Paula's case, it was a bit of a double whammy because she was both desperate to take care of her boys and inspired by her love of cooking.

A lot of people get stuck thinking that they have to invent something incredible, get a degree, or have a ton of money saved up, and that simply isn't true. You just need to look at immigrants who are some of the most successful entrepreneurs in the world. Paula went from sandwich maker and catering business owner to restaurant owner to owning multiple restaurants to television cooking show host to cookbook author to famed celebrity. It didn't happen overnight, and it didn't happen without a lot of hard work, sweat, and tears. But it happened because she determined not to do what she didn't want to do in life and took a chance on doing something she loved and for which she had talent.

What a great example she is of picking yourself up by the bootstraps when you've fallen. Life is not a one-way street, but it is a wild and bumpy ride. You must hang on, enjoy the ride, and look forward to where you're going. Paula Deen spoke from experience when she said, "Change doesn't happen overnight. It starts with the desire, then one small step in the right direction."

You have to open your mind to opportunities, even if it is outside your comfort zone. Start somewhere! Start making "sandwiches" and then let your talent, intuitiveness, and tenacity lead you further and further into your ultimate destiny. Taking action is the key!

You have to move from thoughts about what possibilities are available to you, to conversation, to action. I didn't know what I wanted to do, but somewhat like Paula Deen, I knew what I didn't want to do, and that began to shift my focus to look for opportunities for which I had a passion. Again, this was a paradigm shift for me. The questions I asked myself such as, "What can I do?" and "What do I want to do?" opened doors in my mind which enabled me to begin conversing about it with others, which led to idea generation, and eventually a real business opportunity.

Knowing your AVERSIONS, or what you do *not* want to do, is a great way to force your mind towards the things that you may want to do, or, at least, put you in the mindset of being open to new opportunities. For example, I knew that I did not want to continue to live in Ohio or continue to work for the family business. I also knew that I loved going to spas, helping others and being near the water. So, as you can see, a vision begins to form that you can identify, albeit broadly, but it's there. That first little glimmer of insight may just be the beginning of your future. Think of it like looking through binoculars and the object you're working to focus on is your future self. Patience, focus, and dialing in are key concepts here.

What is it that you have an aversion to and definitely know you don't want to do? Take a moment and begin listing those things. Then, next to that list, begin listing the things you enjoy and those things you love to do. You can always refer back to your list to add other things that come to your mind. For example, I did NOT want to work in our family business any longer and I love going to spas! It may seem trivial, but it's critical to begin identifying the "Do's" and "Do Not's" of YOUR FUTURE FUNNEL™! Like the previous exercise, I've included my personal example. After reviewing what I have outlined, begin listing the things you know you don't want to do and the things you love to do. You may want to ask a friend or family member to help you with this exercise.

KIMMY

Things I Know I Don't Want to Do	Things I Love to Do
I no longer want to live where it's cold	I want to live near water where it's warm
I no longer want to work in the family construction business	I love spas, people, serving others
I don't want to sit in an office alone	I do want to work with others

YOUR FUTURE
FUNNEL™

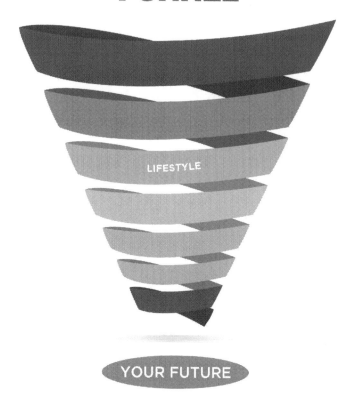

LIFESTYLE

YOUR FUTURE

Chapter 3

Designing Your Life...
It Begins with a Vision
Level 3 – Lifestyle

"Keep only those things that speak to your heart. Then take the plunge and discard all the rest. By doing this, you can reset your life and embark on a new lifestyle."

— Marie Kondo

Question: How do I find a way to live a different lifestyle?

*Y*our desired lifestyle is a significant factor in determining what you will be doing for the remainder of your life. Lifestyle is more than having a nice car and a beautiful home. Lifestyle is what style of life resonates with you. Some people are quite content with a very simple, non-complicated lifestyle that doesn't require much money to support. While others are focused on an elaborate destiny that is filled with exotic travel, multiple homes, luxury cars and possibly very generous philanthropic gestures. Then there are those that fit in between the opposite ends of the lifestyle spectrum I just outlined.

Where are you in this lifestyle spectrum? It is very important to define what amenities you want to have in life since this will be a driving force in determining how much income you will need. It's just as important to determine what kind of activities and climate you desire. You need to differentiate between the tangible and intangible here. You need to think about lifestyle in the sense of where you live, how you work and how you spend your free time. These are more intangible but especially important to identify. In my case, I was living in the wrong city and the wrong state and in the wrong part of the country. The lifestyle that I desired was one without harsh winters and near the water.

When you close your eyes, what lifestyle do you envision for yourself? Be aware of this because that's what you're going towards. That's the outcome for which you are looking. Visualize yourself in the setting that you're trying to create for yourself. You may want to pull pictures from a magazine and put them on a wall or make a vision board, which we will talk about in more depth later. Begin to visualize someone who is living the lifestyle you desire. That could be a famous person, a mentor, or a friend. How will you get there? What is keeping you from that lifestyle?

You may not be able to immediately change where you live, just as I couldn't, but you can begin to change your thought process and consider alternatives. This was a pretty significant issue for me. My "aha" moment came when I was helping a friend with her new business. She had created a business in which hospitals hired her to welcome potential physicians to the city, show them around, highlight the city's most positive and notable benefits, and be persuasive about how grand it would be to live there. I would ride along with her and listen to her sell our city like it was the best place in the world. She was really good at this! The problem was, I didn't share her enthusiasm. But not only did I not share her enthusiasm, I personally didn't like living there.

Yet, **never once had I considered that I had an actual choice in where I lived**. Can we just pause here for a moment? I repeat, I had never considered that I had an actual choice where I lived. It's CRAZY as I think back on this! I never thought about having passion for where I lived. This was a HUGE realization for me and one that would change my life forever!

Hint: It's probably the same type of place where you like to vacation!

Going about our routine of daily living has a subtle way of encapsulating us in the here and now and prevents us from thinking beyond our current existence. Once I actually allowed myself to dream about where I wanted to live, the world got bigger, and my options grew broader. It may not be something you can change immediately but having passion for where you live is important. Do you love where you live? Or do you stay where you are because you were born there, and your family is there? That's exactly what happened to me. I just loved my family so much and didn't allow myself to envision an opportunity to relocate. I would see other people living in cool places and wish that were me. This is one of the most important messages you can take from this book, **a person can live the life of your dreams anywhere you desire**. Why not you?

My friend Angie, a single mom of three, was a banker in my hometown. Like me, she had been there for decades and settled into the Mom, kids, family life and was very active in the community. Once her kids went off to college, she found herself in a bit of a slump. She tried working for different banks and in different positions, but it still wasn't making her happy. Then one day, she had the "tipping point" experience and decided to accept a job in a neighboring city. A bigger city with more to do and closer to her college age kids. It didn't take long for her to get a promotion, meet an amazing boyfriend, and enjoy her new community. But it all started with a *decision* to make a lifestyle change.

Jimmy Buffet is a great example of how a desired lifestyle can actually become your business. He already has all the money he will ever need, but he continues to build his empire in his 70's. His passion and purpose continue as he expands into building extravagant retirement communities for individuals who like the beach vibe in an "It's 5 O'clock Somewhere" atmosphere. Beginning as a budding vocal artist,

Jimmy Buffett's classic hit "Margaritaville" has been enjoyed by young and old alike now for over four decades. The song, debuting on the 1977 "Changes in Latitudes, Changes in Attitudes" album, quickly took on a life of its own, becoming a state of mind and way of life rooted in fun and escapism for those "growing older, but not growing up."

The iconic lifestyle song about life in this euphoric place where days are wasted away nibblin' on sponge cake and watchin' the sun bake has morphed into a global lifestyle brand that currently has more than $4.8 billion in the development pipeline and sees $1.5 billion in annual sales. Buffet's music and desired "beach bum" type lifestyle has parlayed into an empire of iconic music, an expensive merchandise line, hotels, restaurants, casinos, resorts, and retirement communities with an international presence. All built around a lifestyle! He certainly knows what type of lifestyle he wants!!

While you may not ever build your business out of your lifestyle like Mr. Buffet,

it is important to know your desired lifestyle
so you can understand how much money you
will need to maintain it. And, if you're lucky,
you may be able to mix your lifestyle with your
business. Wouldn't it be great to be able to
conduct business while lying on the beach? It's
not impossible, but it will take a considerable
amount of planning and effort to bring to
fruition your desired outcome. Boruch Akbosh
made a brilliant recommendation, "Design
your life in such a way that you would never
need a vacation from it."

In my case, even quitting my first real job
at 20, I knew that my lifestyle choice would
be one where I needed to be free to take care
of my family. I worked at IBM throughout
college and was working at LexisNexis when
I graduated from The University of Dayton
with a Computer Science Degree. My husband
had started a small painting company and was
already living his entrepreneurial career. I was
helping him on evenings and weekends with
the administrative side of the business and

found myself drawn to the freedom of it but also the challenge of keeping things in order and creating processes for him.

Helping my husband with his small business was one of the first indications that I was meant for an entrepreneurial future. In those days, no one even used the word "entrepreneur." It was more like, "He doesn't have a college degree, so he has to work with his hands." It's sad, really, to reflect back and think that although he was a pioneer, there was a stigma associated with "working with your hands." Now, we fully embrace these wild entrepreneurs, trend setters, inventors, and such. Consider how many tech entrepreneurs dropped out of Harvard and Stanford. It's cool to be uniquely you now, thankfully!

So, don't let others bring you down. This is the time to consider your "lifestyle." Let's break that down. YOUR LIFE. YOUR STYLE. If you don't already know, it's your LIFE and you definitely have a STYLE. We are here to help you find it, embrace it, and let it loose.

Jim Rohn said it beautifully, "We all have two choices: we can make a living, or we can design a life." What is your desired lifestyle? Take a few moments to dream. Try to be specific about what you want. Is it a four-day work week or not having to be at a job at the same time every day? Is it that you want to travel or be an independent contractor? Try imaging yourself in your new lifestyle and try it on for size. It's okay if this feels similar to the prior exercises. The idea here is to start to establish a pattern and hone-in on what you want from your life.

In the sample matrix below I have, again, given you an example from my life - things that I didn't like about the lifestyle I was living and what I wanted my lifestyle to become. Take the time now to begin identifying what you don't like about your current lifestyle as well as the lifestyle you desire and make your own lifestyle matrix. I'm sure you've thought about this before. But have you ever taken the time to write it down? If not, now is your chance. Try to be as specific as possible and list as many things as you desire.

KIMMY

What I Don't Like About My Current Lifestyle	The Lifestyle I Want
Driving to shops and restaurants	I want to walk or bike to restaurants and stores
I hate being landlocked	I want to be able to walk to the beach or boat
There is no diversity	I want to live among artists and more diverse cultures

YOUR FUTURE
FUNNEL™

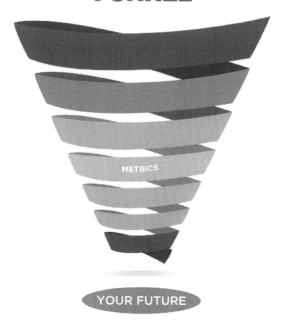

METRICS

YOUR FUTURE

Chapter 4

Let's Do This... It's All In the Planning!
Level 4 - Metrics

"A goal without a plan is just a wish."

— Antoine de Saint-Exupéry

"A clear vision, backed by definite plans, gives you a tremendous feeling of confidence and personal power."

— Brian Tracy

Question: "How do I make a plan if I don't know what I'm going to do?"

*T*o respond to this question, I will direct you back to Your Future Funnel™ we discussed previously. Assuming you have moved through the first three levels of the funnel, Desires, Aversions, and Lifestyle, "Planning" begins in the next level I have entitled "Metrics." Metrics is essentially KNOWING YOUR NUMBERS. It is simply getting real with your reality.

Metrics is basically a term used to describe a method of measuring something. What's most important here is to get really real with where you are financially. Undercapitalization is a huge contributing factor to most business failures and similarly, personal bankruptcy. Even if you're financially well off or comfortable and have savings or investors for your business, you must know where you stand and have a complete understanding of all the ways you can free up cash, capital, or investments.

If you're not good with money and don't have a decent track record with managing your finances, now is the time to stop and take a good look at this aspect of your life. The predictor of future behavior is current behavior. That is not to say that you cannot change, because that is the point of this book, but it takes clarity and focus to move on to the next level.

Even as I write this, I know I can do better and am always working at it. We waste a lot of money and therefore opportunity when we don't have a financial plan or work within a budget. The lines just get blurred, and we sometimes spend mindlessly without realizing how much lost opportunity comes when we squander our resources.

Metrics will be critical for any future endeavor. What I mean by metrics is how much are you spending now? How much do you have saved? How much will it cost to allow you to start this journey? How much debt do you have? These questions are absolutely essential to answer before moving to the next step.

Use a personal financial worksheet to help you dive deeper and get your arms around your finances. We will discuss this more in Chapters 5 and 6, but this is when you also need to start evaluating your relationships and any that drain or strain your financial health.

Once you've established all of your monthly expenses, monthly income, assets, and liabilities, you can move on. This first step should really be "where you are right this minute." Using an automobile analogy, how much gas is in your tank? How efficiently is your car running?

Next, if needed or not, identify things you can reduce or eliminate to free up cash. For example, take on a roommate, sell your house, pick up an extra job to reduce credit card debt, eliminate gym memberships and cable, sell your car and carpool, etc. You need to begin to find the right path to afford to take the next step. Even if you're well to do, seek more clarity and reduce the clutter in your financial picture. Look at the interest rates you're paying, the returns on your investments, your insurance premiums, etc.

If you need to reduce your debt and you're thinking, for example, of opening a deli, then work at a deli and help pay off some bills. You can combine the two for sure. If you cannot get past this step, you should probably not go into business for yourself and that's okay. This step is for you to determine your options. If you're looking to spend more time by the beach and want to have weekends off and write a book, then maybe you eliminate some of your expenses, work weekday evenings at a restaurant, and then write on the weekends. The point is, it's your choice! You are not stuck on the treadmill of life. You are driving your own destiny. The trick is to use the dashboard to read the gauges and understand what you have to work with and what is feasible.

Another very important factor to consider is how much time you realistically have to spend on your desired life. If you are a busy parent or caring for a loved one, you have to be honest and objective about your time. Do you really have the time to give to create the life you desire? While creating a plan to help you reach your desired life is essential, it also has to be realistic. Are you able to commit the necessary time to make it happen? There may also be other factors that take up your time such as a hobby, commitments to immediate or extended family, etc. All these factors must be considered.

The amount of time you take to fulfill your desire to own your own business or make a new career move must also be part of the Metrics you consider. For example, if you are making and selling candles, you must factor in your time like an employee to make sure you are still making a profit. In addition to the cost of raw materials, equipment, and supplies, how much time does it take you to make the candles, market them, and sell them? As simple as this principle may seem, many business owners don't factor in their own time when producing and selling a product. It is not uncommon for business owners to be working for very little money when they break it down to an hourly wage. In fact, a lot of people waste years owning their own business and running themselves ragged when they could have spent less time working for someone else and have more time and money for their family.

There was a wonderful massage therapist at our spa. At one time she actually owned her own spa, where she also performed the massages. When I met her, she was physically, spiritually, and financially drained. She was very stressed out and unhappy as a business owner. Shortly after closing her business and working for my spa, she told me how much happier she was, and she was making more money than she had in a very long time. Sometimes owning your own business is not the answer, despite what you may think. Understanding your current financial means, your real desires and associated cost and opportunities is a critical part of YOUR FUTURE FUNNEL™.

When my husband and I were building our first business, a painting company, I was working full time, had health benefits and a steady income, and he was able to take some risks. We knew that if he didn't get paid on a job right away, we could still pay the rent, utilities, and other financial obligations. If you have a partner, this is one way to carefully step out and begin to take a risk. It wasn't long before my husband's painting company really got busy, and I was working before and after my "day job" to help keep his billing and administrative duties under control. I speak about this type of entrepreneurship as "zero entry." You aren't taking a huge leap, taking out a huge loan, or putting a lot at risk, but it's still very scary because there is no real fall back plan this way. A lot of people say they want to work for themselves but if you're not really sure, a service business could be a good place to start.

If you're looking to change careers, this is a good time to evaluate all of the "costs" involved. Oftentimes, travel, dry cleaning, dining out, childcare, and a host of other things can really add up when you're working for someone else. All of those expenses really need to be analyzed carefully. It might appear as if you're making a lot of money per your salary, but when you start breaking down the costs in both time and money, you may find out that you're not really making as much as you think and you're unhappy doing it. This is something Henry David Thoreau realized and explained in his 1854 book, Walden, *"The cost of a thing is the amount of what I will call life, which is required to be exchanged for it, immediately or in the long run."*

Here are some real-life examples to help you think through how best to design the life you really want:

Me: When I decided to move from Ohio to South Carolina and open up a Woodhouse Spa, I had to work with my husband, accountant, and financial planner. It would take a huge bit of our savings and all of the equity in our real estate to afford to buy and build the spa. It was a huge risk and one that put my family at risk. However, my husband would continue running our construction company and I had the security of that as a backup plan. That was key for me. We found a way to minimize or manage the risk by understanding where we were and what it would take to open a new business. I couldn't have done it any other way. Unfortunately, others have failed by getting in over their head and not having a plan. I understand that pain because I, too, have failed at business and lost money. It happens, but you want to try your best to mitigate the risks and the best way to do this is to have a good plan.

Denise: Denise doesn't have a lot of cash free to start her new career and she doesn't want to borrow a lot at her age. She doesn't have much debt but realized she could reduce her expenses if she rode her bike to work and could increase her income if she opened a small business of her own. Due to her work moving through the FUTURE FUNNEL, Denise ruled out expensive franchises that would require a large amount of capital investment and a long lease, but considered opening up a business by adding an additional certification as an Esthetician and Laser Technician so she could do lasers and facials. Denise is properly using the FUTURE

FUNNEL to be realistic about what is the right fit for her both financially and passionately.

Beth: Beth is young and has a small savings account. She and her fiancé own a home and have little debt. Beth worked through the FUTURE FUNNEL and ruled out anything that resembled a corporate 8-5 job but did realize that teaching was a very viable option for her. Teaching would allow her to have job security, utilize her passion for children, and give her summers and holidays to be with her family. She will also be able to have a good work/life balance when she decides to have children. Additionally, she can coach the sailing or running team and take students on skiing trips. Another option available to her is to tutor students in her free time to bring in extra income.

This is the power of applying the FUTURE FUNNEL to your life. It helps you to truly think through what you want your life to be and how you want to live it.

YOUR FUTURE
FUNNEL™

PREPARATION

YOUR FUTURE

Chapter 5

Order Is Important: Ready, Aim, Fire – Not Ready, Fire, Aim
Level 5 – Preparation

"An hour of planning can save you 10 hours of doing."

— Dale Carnegie

*R*eady, aim, fire! Not ready, fire, aim. It's all in the planning. Hopefully in the previous chapters you've identified your passion, resources, and opportunities and know your reality. And you've done some planning. Now it's time to prepare! This is where you discover the opportunities available to you and begin developing a strategic plan that can eventually be fully implemented at the appropriate time in your journey. If you want to be wise and strategic in your business then follow the advice from the Dale Carnegie quote above and also pay attention to the wisdom of Abraham Lincoln when he said, "Give me six hours to chop down a tree and I will spend the first four sharpening the ax."

By moving through the first three levels of the funnel you may have discovered three or four opportunities that you will want to investigate. By completing the fourth level of the funnel, you now are clear on what you can and cannot afford to do. At this point, you're now ready to begin delving into research on your future plans and talking to people that have experienced what you are now viewing as potential opportunities. It's very important that you AIM before FIRING. A lot of times people get very excited to go off and do something but fail to do the hard work it takes to get started. If you FIRE before AIMING... well, you know what happens - YOU MISS THE MARK!

I was at an entrepreneur event called One Million Cups where there was a speaker who had presented his product, BevBoy, a floating koozie, on Shark Tank. He had been humiliated by "Mr. Wonderful," on the show, but was fortunate enough to strike a deal with Daymond John. He went on to sell thousands of floating koozies and then expand his business with things for which he had a passion. At the end of his presentation at One Million Cups, the moderator asked the audience, "Who here is trying to launch a product or business?" Three people stood up. One of them was a man starting a camera business. He said, "I just started my business and have launched out on my own. I'm looking for more people interested in my services." The moderator then said to the audience, "Okay, before you leave today, three of you have to give him your business card and three of you have to connect with him to tell him of someone you know who can use his services." I said to my eighteen-year-old son, who had just started his own drone business and was with me at the event, "I want you to go up to him, introduce yourself, and give him your business card." My eighteen-year-old son went up to him, introduced himself and told him about the business he had just started. It's important to show up locally and speak up about what you're looking to do. People want to help, especially entrepreneurs. Yes, you may be humiliated on national television, but only if you're lucky!

It's a great idea to check out local events and go to them and network. Support others and ask them how they got started and speak up about being in a rut and trying to find something new. It be really hard at first, trust me, I know! At this particular event, I was nearly 20 years older than most of the "kids" there, but I wanted to hear the speaker and teach my son something and I'm glad I did.

You may be fearful or intimidated because you're considering a business you know nothing about. I can identify with you! Not only did I not know anything about the spa business, but I didn't really know anything about franchising.

I was at the spa one day when I still lived in Dayton and heard a guest talking about the Woodhouse Day Spa being a franchise. That was actually when the franchise light bulb went off for me. In my wildest dreams, I had never considered owning a franchise and frankly was ignorant and somewhat dismissive of the concept. But I eventually decided to take a closer look and filled out the application at www.ownawoodhouse.com. I also reached out to the owner of my local Woodhouse Day Spa and took him up on his offer to meet with me and answer any of my questions. That day would forever change my life in so many ways.

The important thing here is that I started with passion, I was open to ideas, took action steps, and asked questions. I also knew what I didn't want to do. Again, I knew that I did not want to continue to live in Ohio and work for the family business. And I knew that I loved going to spas, helping others, and being near the water. As you can see, a vision begins to form that you can identify, albeit broadly, but it's there. That little first glimmer of your future.

As I previously mentioned, I actually had some well-meaning friends who initially talked me out of moving forward with the Woodhouse Spa franchise. As a result, I sat on the idea for a while because I allowed them to talk me out of it.

I allowed myself to listen to people that focused on the negative aspects of the idea. However, after idling for some time, I had a resurgence of motivation and said to myself, "It can't hurt anything for me to fly down there and talk to the Woodhouse Day Spa franchisors." So, I did. It was such a huge operation! I thought, "There is no way I could do this by myself." But the franchise route made it less intimidating. Talking to someone that made the process work was what catapulted me into franchise ownership. I found a way to make it approachable for me. But I had to take those first investigative steps toward what I thought I wanted to do to determine if it was going to be feasible for me. I learned through that experience that there is always a way to make it less terrifying.

As I recall my own experience, it took a lot of courage to call a highly successful owner of a Woodhouse Day Spa to ask if I can come talk to him about his business. To be totally honest, I was actually terrified to do it. It sounded like a crazy idea to me. I thought he was some big important person that I would never be able to reach on the phone, let alone meet in person. However, the very opposite was true. He turned out to be a very approachable person who has been a great mentor to me, thank you Chris Mann!

What I learned from that experience is that I should never allow myself to be intimidated. And I'm going to pass that advice on to you. Don't ever allow yourself to be intimidated by a successful person. You will find they are often the individuals who are the most willing to talk to you and help you become successful. The reason for this is that most of them have been exactly where you are today. They can identify with your fears, hesitations, and apprehensions. They have been through the fire and have come out on the other side and they will likely be the right person to teach you how to go through the fire without getting burned.

I have found there is always something out there for what you want to do. Some people have started businesses from scratch and have been remarkably successful. However, I'm convinced that if I were to have started from scratch, I would have failed. I would not have known what I was doing. The franchise gave me a formula for success, and I discovered they are a very viable option for people who want to get started but don't know how.

Read and Network with Others

Another particularly important aspect of this Investigation level is to read, read, read. Obtain and digest as much information as you can possibly find so that you will know what questions to ask when you have the opportunity to get in front of an expert. In this age of information there is no excuse to not spend large amounts of time researching your field of interest and you will likely find it is more fun than laborious because it's a subject that already intrigues you.

The more knowledge you have, the better your questions will be, which will lead to much more meaningful conversations. It may also expose parts of the business that you are more interested in than others. For example, I love owning the spa and coming up with new ways to be efficient, make guests happy, and expand our product line. However, I don't so much care for the busy work of making the schedules, human resources, inventory, etc. I love the business of the business, but my passion is at a high level in developing the spa, opening another spa, etc. This is why I have invested in a very strong General Manager and have surrounded myself with a great team. This will be discussed in more detail in the next chapter when we look at the Action step of Your Future Funnel™. But at this point, try to pinpoint what it is you like about a business or career so that you can get to the position for which you have the most passion. You won't necessarily start in this position, but you will get there with the proper planning and preparation. Just like you'd expect of your employees, you have to be willing to start at the bottom and do every job yourself at the beginning. Although I do not necessarily have a passion for every position within my company, I have done them all myself, which enables me to understand what I'm expecting from my team as we grow. I have also come to realize I must continuously evolve and embrace change as needed.

It is very possible that as you read about local or regional businesses in your area of interest, you will find networking opportunities that arise, a conference focusing on your business niche, or other interesting happenings around town that will get you in front of the right people. Don't be hesitant to attend these events and begin talking to people. Invite someone to go out to coffee and chat.

It is also possible through the process of networking with others in your field of interest and talking with experts, you will find someone who you will consider to be a mentor. Mentoring doesn't have to be a formal process. In fact, most successful mentoring relationships are quite informal and happen organically rather than being forced. When you find someone who serves that role of mentor for you, it is especially important to capitalize on the value of that relationship. Don't just listen to them, but also watch them. Much can be learned by watching someone model an attribute, characteristic, or skill. Some things are better "caught" than "taught." Seeking out opportunities to discuss and learn is easy to accomplish, and it can have a monumental impact on your future success.

There will be many qualified and excellent business and life coaches to choose from as you make your way through the funnel. But make sure you check references and vet them. Talking about your desires and passions with an experienced mentor or coach is like dropping a tiny piece of sand into a bucket. Every time you do, it starts to accumulate, and the big picture then begins to take shape. It's a great opportunity to express your ideas, obtain feedback and advice, expand your horizons, and solidify your direction.

Be Nice to People

Another particularly important point to keep in mind is, as my Daddy used to say, "Be nice to people on the way up, because you might meet them again on your way down." You may become phenomenally successful, but there is no guarantee your success will last indefinitely. There is always the possibility of something happening that would cause you to once again need some of those people you encountered on your way up.

When the economy took a nosedive in 2008, our construction company's biggest clients began pulling their purchase orders and canceling scheduled jobs. When that happened, we immediately went to our strategic mentor. After some brainstorming with our strategist, he came up with a recommended tactic to help us through the economic downturn so we could remain solvent. Having his support and council enabled us to make some very important decisions to keep the company profitable during a very scary time. Unfortunately, many of our competitors did not survive the downturn, but we were one of the fortunate companies that came through that recession and eventually we were able to make up lost ground on the other side.

But we survived only because we maintained all the relationships with the people that originally were instrumental in our success. My point here is that you must have the right people around you to help you strategically and in many other ways when you are thrown a curve ball because you can rest assured, there will be many curve balls that come at you from all directions during the lifetime of your business. There will always be business hurricanes, tornadoes and wildfires that occur. Notice I didn't say "may" occur, I said "will" occur. You can count on it! You must be ready for it by maintaining all your business relationships and simply being nice to people.

I say all this not to scare you away from business, but rather to encourage you to always keep yourself surrounded by the right people and not burn bridges. You will certainly run into people who won't treat you fairly and who will take advantage of you. But you must decide how you will react to those situations. Always try to keep all relationships in good standing.

Proper Capitalization Cannot Be Overstated

A very large part of your planning is to be prepared financially. Undercapitalization is the number one reason businesses fail. So, start small and build your business within your financial means. Many who aspire to business ownership have to start small to gain business experience and also because they have limited capital. I've often recommended to people that they begin with something financially feasible. Many have gotten their feet wet in business by starting a small lawn mowing business. Then, when it's financially viable, they hire someone else to mow lawns with them as the business expands. However, expansion has to be intentionally based on your budget, not on your desire to become a bigger business at a fast pace. You must be able to sustain your overhead, including the wages of the people working for you.

Early in our first business, a painting company, we completed a job for a customer, but she didn't pay us the $4,000 balance for the work that was completed. This put us in an exceedingly difficult position because we needed that money to make payroll for our employees. It became very awkward because it happened to be a friend of a family member and we had to engage the help of that family member to resolve the matter. The good news is that she finally came through at the last minute with the payment and we were able to meet our payroll obligations. However, this type of thing often happens, especially with new businesses who do not yet have substantial cash flow. They usually run on very tight budgets. You can't start big right out of the gate. You have to make sure you have enough capital to maintain your overhead as well as knowing you can financially support your employees before you hire them.

You've probably heard it before, "Failing to plan is planning to fail." Benjamin Franklin's wise words still ring true today. But you don't plan just so you won't fail, you plan so you can comprehensively understand the foundation of your desired business. Not planning is like not checking the gasoline, oil, and battery in your car and not having a GPS with you before taking a trip across the country. You have to plan for your trip. First, you need to know your final destination, then you will need to have enough gas, make sure the oil is clean and full, determine if the battery is good enough to continue to hold a charge, make sure there is plenty of good tread on your tires, make sure you have your GPS, and be certain you have enough money to get you to your destination. To carry the car analogy further, in business you have to plan for a flat tire, for replacing the brakes, and for fixing the cracked windshield. Sometimes you will have to do these things in spite of the fact that you have some clients or customers who haven't yet paid you.

Activity

I encourage you to put into practice what we've discussed. Here are a couple of suggestions.

1. Identify a person or organization you admire and interview that person or someone from that organization. Find out what their biggest obstacle was to get to where they are today.

2. Research the three most successful and three failures in the business vertical in which you are most interested. Set an appointment to talk with these individuals. Find out from each of these conversations what they would do differently if they were to do things all over again.

In response to the second activity above, I can offer my own experience. If I were to do things over again, I would have taken a job as a Woodhouse Day Spa hospitality team member to better understand the entire business before purchasing my own franchise. As I look back, I believe it was more of a pride issue that prevented me from pursuing that kind of a job prior to ownership. If I would have done that, I would have had a much more productive first year in business. So, I encourage you to not let pride become a factor in preventing you from taking all the necessary steps in completing a very thorough due diligence. Your future business is very important. Make sure you take the time to do the proper amount of investigative work and planning. Taking more time on this step will increase the likelihood of earlier success in your endeavor.

YOUR FUTURE
FUNNEL™

ACTION

YOUR FUTURE

Chapter 6

Having A Winning Team
Level 6 – Action

"It takes two flints to make a fire."

— Louisa May Alcott

*H*ere is a wise piece of advice. Surround yourself with those who share and support your vision. I have learned the importance of this through experience.

The bold decision to leave our long-standing family business, move to Charleston, South Carolina, and start my own Woodhouse Day Spa franchise was not made in a void. On the contrary, I had many sit-down conversations with my husband about my vision and the costs related to venturing out in a brand-new line of business. We discussed not only the monetary cost, but also how it was going to impact our relationship. I had to ask the tough question, "Are you willing to continue to be the sole breadwinner while I go off on this tangent." And, fortunately, he was incredibly supportive of the plan! Being a born entrepreneur, he was all in from the very beginning.

But this decision wasn't just affecting the two of us. I also sat down with my children. One had just left for college, one was a high school senior, and one was an eighth grader.

As you can imagine, this was a life changing decision for them as well, especially our high school senior and eighth grader. That meant they would be leaving their life-time friends to go to a community where they had never been to attend a new school and make new friends. It was imperative for me to include my entire family in this discussion because if you don't have a supportive family, it could have serious ramifications.

After many, many conversations and questions as a family unit, and after performing our due diligence to determine if this was a financially sound move, the decision was made. We moved our entire family to Charleston to begin a new chapter of life in a geographic area where there were more tropical-like days than chilly days.

By this time in our lives, we had been in business for nearly 25 years and knew that my husband could continue to run the construction company. So, we knew we would be able to feed our children and pay our bills while stepping into this new entrepreneurial territory. That was especially important to us.

Unfortunately, some people don't have the financial support they need to make these kinds of big steps. Or some might have a spouse that says, "No way, you're on your own!" I can't overly stress the importance of having the financial stability you need as well as the support from your family when considering such a big lifestyle change. You need to know who is on your team, and that includes family members.

Sometimes you may have family members that advise you not to follow your dream. That doesn't necessarily mean you have to follow their advice, but you should seriously consider the sincere thoughts of those that care most about you. If you have people who are important to you trying to steer you in another direction, you ultimately still have to make a decision based on what you truly believe is the best for you.

When my husband and I were first thinking of starting our painting company back in 1990 we sought advice from our family. I was a junior in college at the time studying computer science while my husband was working to pay the bills. Because my father was already in business as a general contractor, we decided to ask for his advice about starting a painting business. His advice was very straight forward, "You don't want to do that. You will need at least $15,000 in the bank." Well, we didn't have $15,000 at the time, nor did we have the ability to save that much money in a short period of time. So, you can imagine how discouraging those words were to a young couple with big aspirations of business ownership.

In hindsight, I believe my father was giving us very good information based on his experience. However, this was something my husband really wanted to do, and he was determined to work for himself. So, we moved forward with starting a painting business with really no start-up capital and it eventually became a successful business venture, however, it was difficult, and we learned my father was correct – having $15,000 would have helped a lot. Let's just say, we were, ahem, undercapitalized.

My take-away from that experience is that if you don't have a family member who is supportive, then you really need to talk to your winning team to figure out what your strategy is going to be and how to overcome the obstacles that are concerning to that family member. Don't be upset with someone that is negative because they are very likely sincerely concerned about your best interest and potential success. But consider their comments seriously and probe further on their concerns. If I would have put my pride aside, talked more with my father, and asked for his help in planning, I'm sure he would have taught me so much more and saved us from many "on the job" lessons.

It's important to know which family members or friends are or are not going to be part of your support team. Of course, it would be nice if all your family members and friends would be supportive, but usually not everybody will be on board, and that's okay. We continued on with our plan to start a painting business despite the fact that my dad, whom we both highly respected, told us it wasn't a good idea at that time in our lives. And he was not too pleased when I quit my corporate job to help my husband with the business. But we did it anyway. We still loved and respected my father, but we were convinced we could make it happen and we did just that.

So, you don't always have to have everybody's 100% approval. Just make sure you are wise about the decisions you make and be certain you have done your due diligence. At the beginning of our business, I was able to secure a corporate job that paid our bills while my husband began building the business. When it looked like I could transition into helping with the business, I made that move and we continued to evolve into other businesses that were very successful.

One thing we did do correctly was to make sure to not take on too much debt. We lived in a modest house and drove modest cars to avoid having a lot of overhead. This is why the Metrics level of Your Future Funnel™ is so important. Every dollar counts when starting a business or new career opportunity. "A penny saved is a penny earned." It took me a long time to really grasp what this meant. Although Franklin never actually said it quite this way, the message still stands. Money that you don't spend or that you save, is money you can use!

What about when a spouse is not supportive of your business venture? That can certainly be tricky. I have seen situations where a spouse is not supportive of a business venture, and it makes it much more difficult on the person running the business. Sometimes the biggest issue in these circumstances is the lack of emotional and moral support. It can become quite discouraging. There are also times when a spouse can be somewhat antagonistic while they are just waiting in the wings to say, "I told you so." Or a spouse may be very adamant about not having any financial connection to the business idea. Certainly, it's not an ideal situation, but you have to honor their perspective. It's important to get really clear about who is on your side and who is not on your side and what someone is willing to do or not willing to do to help you. By gaining such clarity you can better define your relationship when it comes to business, thereby, creating less of a chance of disrupting the personal side of your relationship.

There will always be naysayers out there. But you have to remove those negative obstacles and voices of defeat from your business. By proper planning and preparation, you can find ways around the potential obstacles announced by those naysayers. If you have done the proper planning and preparation, you will be surrounded by resources that will help you battle through the difficult times and overcome any barrier that may seem to prevent you from succeeding. After you have completed a very objective and honest due diligence and have decided entrepreneurship or business ownership is your future, then choose to surround yourself with positive people that are leading the type of life that you're interested in pursuing, versus continuing to surround yourself with people who may be consistently telling you what you can't do instead of offering solutions on how you can do it.

This doesn't mean you completely cut off others who don't support you, but it may mean you don't spend as much time with them. I have quotes posted in various places to motivate me, but one of my favorite quotes is, "Show me your friends, and I'll show you your future." Those words are so true. Surrounding yourself with positive successful people may be the catalyst which propels you into success.

Moving from Ohio to Charleston didn't come without some emotional struggles. I had great friends in Ohio and a great life there. That's where I raised my children. But when I was approaching 45, I began thinking about becoming an empty nester and what chapter two of our lives was going to be. After I made the move to Charleston, I noticed a cultural difference. The energy of Charleston was extremely collaborative and entrepreneurial. There was a unique business energy that I had never before experienced, and people were all about how they can help one another become more successful. It's amazing what a springboard that has become.

Whether you are in a small town or a bigger city really isn't the point. Every town has people that will want to see you succeed. There may be some communities that focus on this more than others, but you have to find the right people where you live. And, if you can't find the right people, you may have to consider relocating to a place where entrepreneurship and business is valued and promoted. Having passion for where you live is important. A change of scenery can really open up new ideas and motivation. Unique and creative collaboration is key in any life or career change.

The concept of Your Future Funnel™ is to help you get clarity around these collaborative efforts that likely exist where you live. Your Future Funnel™ is like using a pair of binoculars and adjusting the lenses so you can see far and clear enabling you to become very focused. I wish someone would have informed me of the importance of collaboration years ago. I knew there were other business owners and entrepreneurs out there, I just didn't know how to harness the spirit of collaboration to create a mutually beneficial relationship.

Almost every city in the world now has many organizations whether in person or remotely to help you connect with other entrepreneurs and coaches. For example, in Charleston, The Hatch Tribe was established by Hilary Johnson as a one-stop shop for connections, resources, and training to help individuals build a better business. We also have The Harbor Entrepreneur Center in Charleston which is an accelerator program with this mission: "To create collision among the entrepreneur community. By nature, entrepreneurs are problem solvers. We believe by connecting the thinkers, the doers, and visionaries we will support the economic vitality of the region."

There are also programs at your local Chamber of Commerce, colleges, and universities. One resource called, 1 Million Cups, is based on the notion that entrepreneurs discover solutions and engage with their communities over a million cups of coffee. Another opportunity developed by the Ewing Marion Kauffman Foundation in 2012 is a free program designed to educate, engage, and inspire entrepreneurs around the country and is now in more than 180 communities. Make sure to check your own community to see if there is a 1 Million Cups organization nearby or other similar programs to accelerate the business community.

I have found, as have so many others, these groups are not only a place to learn great business strategies, but it is also a place where you can grow your business by networking with other business owners and entrepreneurs. No matter what kind of small business you're in, that kind of networking is so critical. While everyone there is desiring to build and grow their own business, it is also a very supportive, helpful, and encouraging environment for any entrepreneur at any level.

You never know where certain business relationships may lead you. I will tell a quick story about where a networking relationship took me after I moved to Charleston. I have a friend who was, and still is, involved with Impact X at the College of Charleston, an experiential learning project that involves an iterative process of developing and testing a business model for a startup that makes a profit, while making a difference. The program is designed to help students become entrepreneurs. Before he was my friend, he posted on Facebook something about his involvement with the program and I responded with a complimentary comment and indicated I was interested in learning more about the program.

To my surprise, he extended an invitation to me to come to the college to learn more about the program, which I readily accepted. Interestingly, that was something the "old me" would never have done. Through that visit I eventually began to serve as a mentor in the program during a weekly class. From there I became a judge for the student presentations and then an investor in the program, enabling me to develop a very good relationship with the founder of the program.

Because of my involvement and commitment to the Impact X program, I was eventually asked to serve on the Board of Governors for the College of Charleston, an honor I never anticipated. However, I am very thankful for the opportunity to now serve in this capacity and give back in a small way to the community that has served me so well. I think this is a great example of how a small effort in networking, in this case a reply to a Facebook post, can result in something you never imagined. Thank you, Stuart Williams (https://www.inplaceimpact.com/).

As we conclude this chapter, allow me to recap. First, I believe it is particularly important to know who is on your side and is supporting you in your business endeavor. Which family members and which friends can you count on for emotional and moral support as well as advice when you need it? Second, it is imperative to seek out and develop relationships that will help you grow and develop your business at a faster pace than you could by yourself. Find a mentor that will be willing to work with you in a developmental capacity. They are out there and many of them are very willing to assist others in becoming successful.

Who do you admire? Who has had the success you are looking to obtain in your own career or journey into business ownership? Interestingly, I had an employee come to me with a question the other day. She is a very lovely person who just started working at the spa four or five months ago. She had just graduated from college with a degree in marketing. I think she was somewhat nervous to talk to me, which I find hard to believe. But I also remember feeling nervous approaching other people and striking up a conversation, so I can totally relate to her. She politely asked if I had a few minutes to talk to which I replied, "Yes, of course." We sat down and she said, "I really admire you for the business you are building here, and I would like to do something similar. Would you mind telling me how you got into this business and what advice you might have for me?" I was more than happy to tell her my story and give her some ideas about what she can do in the future to develop her own business.

I think not allowing your fears to hold you back from seeking the advice from someone else who is doing what you want to do is not only brave, but also imperative in order to follow your dreams. Eleanor Roosevelt said, "You gain strength, courage, and confidence by every experience in which you really stop to look fear in the face. You are able to say to yourself, 'I lived through this horror. I can take the next thing that comes along.' You must do the thing you think you cannot do." You don't have to be intimidated by fear!

Find out how others did it and what obstacles they faced in the process. I can't emphasize that enough. You can learn so much simply by asking good questions and usually people who are successful are happy to share information with you. And, if you find someone who doesn't want to share their time and expertise with you, they probably aren't the right person with whom you should be networking. Just politely thank them and find someone else who will give you the time you deserve.

Networking is sort of an odd thing to do at first, especially if you are introverted by nature. I know this because it was outside my comfort zone. But after you have done it for a while, it becomes much more comfortable. In business you eventually come to understand that if you don't network you won't have customers, and nothing is quite as terrifying as not having customers to keep your business moving in the right direction. You will find that a little desperation can be quite motivational, and it can actually make you a better entrepreneur.

YOUR FUTURE
FUNNEL™

LEGACY

YOUR FUTURE

Chapter 7

Happy Ending: It's Not What You're Thinking But It's Time To Think About It
Level 7 – Legacy

"The idea is to die young as late as possible."

— Ashley Montagu

"My legacy is that I stayed on course...from the beginning to the end, because I believed in something inside me."

— Tina Turner

*W*e have all experienced a great party, or weekend, or vacation that left us feeling like we wished it would never end. Wouldn't it be great if those feel-good, exhilarating times lasted forever? Well, unfortunately, the old adage is actually a reality, "all good things must come to an end." But knowing that and planning for it can certainly make your ending something you can be happy about. In fact, there is also some exhilaration in knowing you are creating a retirement lifestyle that will be worry-free from a financial perspective. You may recall the Introduction to this book began with this question, "How does this story end?" Alas, we have come full circle. Let's talk more about the end of your story.

If you are younger, retirement may seem like it's a long way away from where you are today. You may not have it yet in your sites. But if you are closer to middle age or beyond it is undoubtedly playing a much bigger role in your thoughts and planning. No matter your age, if you are making money, you should be planning for retirement. Keep in mind, retirement doesn't have to have an age attached to it.

According to the dictionary, retirement means to "withdraw from one's position or occupation or from active working life." Think about this. You can achieve retirement when you have sources of income that do not have to be earned by working. Retirement and the term "financial independence" are often used interchangeably.

So, let's chat about that for a minute. Focus on the key words in this sentence: *"...when you have sources of income that do not have to be earned by working."* This is the real meaning of retirement and what we call "Passive Income." This is the most critical part of your future funnel™ because it is this part of planning that allows you to retire comfortably. You cannot rely on the government, a pension, or a retirement plan to do all of the work. You need to make sure that you have multiple sources of income and diversification in order to make sure you are able to retire.

I know of employees at "Blue Chip" companies who retired from management with millions in retirement funds. No doubt you have probably read stories of the schoolteacher or librarian who lived modestly and managed to save over a million dollars. The point is, with proper planning and budgeting, anything is achievable. As nice as it is to have a big house and fancy cars, sometimes it's those exact purchases that will prevent you from achieving true wealth and independence. We all know the legendary story of Warren Buffet, the billionaire who still lives in the same house he had before he became uber successful.

Warren is all about compound interest. There's an important lesson to be learned in the basic understanding of interest. Obviously, there is interest you PAY (mortgage, car loan, school loan, credit card, etc.) and then there is interest you EARN (investments, savings, etc.). Both need to be carefully managed. Having a robust understanding of the impact of the interest you pay and the effect of compounding interest you earn will have a significant impact on your legacy. In simple terms, compounding interest happens when you begin to be paid interest on your interest. When this takes place, your investments begin to grow at a more rapid pace and the compounding effect can be very substantial to your financial portfolio. While I am not a financial expert, I do know there is great advice readily available to those who need it and will seek it out. In fact, if you want to design a life with a happy ending, it is imperative to have a financial expert or advisor as part of your winning team.

So, how do you do it? Well, we just took time in the previous chapters to explain how to find your passion and purpose and the importance of surrounding yourself with a winning team and mentors. So, you should be able to tap into your network to find opportunities to create passive income.

Real Estate is probably one of the most obvious and most utilized methods. Rental income from properties can provide a stable and solid retirement plan. You may decide to sell a business you've been running or create a new business that can run without you. You may work for a great employer who offers profit sharing. If that is the case, it is always wise to maximize that investment and learn to live without the extra cash from the get-go. If your employer offers matching contributions to your 401K, take advantage of that free money.

There are great money managers and investment apps where you can begin investing small amounts that can really add up over time. The one thing you cannot do is do nothing and expect things to fall into place. Planning for how your final years will go is particularly important and will help you budget better and spend less because you'll be thinking about your future, and it may keep you from making wasteful purchases or spending needlessly. Hopefully, by this point in the book, you know that you want to remove as much debt as possible by the time you retire. Ideally, by that time you should be completely debt free. Your house and cars should be paid in full, and you should have enough money to take care of yourself even if you live to be 100. The important thing is that no matter where you are in Your Future Funnel™, you're thinking and planning for your retirement years now. The younger you are, the easier this is because of time.

Disability insurance is also something to consider. Statistically, one in seven people ages 35-65 can expect to become disabled for five years or longer. If you become disabled, you must have safeguards in place to know you will be able to afford to take care of yourself and get the help you need. For some that will be a short and long-term disability insurance policy. Others may have the financial ability to be self-insured by having enough financial assets to sustain them through a long-term or permanent disability. It is always a very good idea to consult a tax specialist, financial planner, or wealth management advisor to make sure you've thought through where you are now and where you want to be in the future.

Some individuals reading this book may be wondering how you can do this when you're living paycheck to paycheck. I promise you that it can be done. Take one step at a time, adjust your lifestyle accordingly and focus on your Happy Ending, because no one likes a sad ending, right?!

A Lasting Legacy – Parting Gifts That Are Part Of You

William James said, "The great use of life is to spend it for something that will outlast it." Someday we will all graduate from retirement. What then? That is, what happens to us after we are gone? It's not all that pleasant to think about but it's the final stop in Your Future Funnel™ and ultimately will reveal your WHY. Why did you work so hard and what did your passion create? Did you purposefully leave a mark on those who matter most to you and are they left with a gift, whether tangible or intangible or hopefully both?

How do you want to be remembered? Have you taken the proper steps to help your loved ones by making sure you have a will, a living will, a trust, instructions on how and where you want to be buried? These things may seem so far away or too difficult to address but the alternatives are always harder on those left behind.

My father had a stroke at 65 and had to immediately retire from running his construction company 7 days a week. He and my uncle had a plan, but it was outdated and full of missing links. While we were grateful for the amazing financial planning my father had done, there wasn't a plan for business succession, which ultimately caused the business to fade as my uncle's health declined.

If my father and uncle had gotten together more often to update their plan, groom and hire a replacement CEO, and include their family, things would have been easier and turned out better for everyone involved. That's the thing about planning, it's hard to get motivated and so easy to put off. But the hard work pays off and can benefit those you love the most. Money left on the table could easily be reallocated efficiently with the right legacy planning. It is important to surround yourself with trusted advisors such as an estate planning attorney, a financial planner, and a very good tax expert. Together, these individuals can help you maximize your investments and pay the least amount in taxes as legally possible. That means there will be more assets to pass on to your designated heirs or the charity of your choice.

The point is your legacy is important. What you leave behind and those to whom you rely on to execute it deserve your attention now.

Exactly what does it mean to leave a legacy? In simple terms, a legacy is passed from one generation to the next and often refers to gifts of money or property. People leave a legacy to ensure their loved ones will be taken care of when they're gone, and that they will always be remembered with love.

With careful planning throughout Your Future Funnel™, you can ensure that you are leaving your life's gift in capable and loving hands. If you start thinking about it before you need to think about it, you'll be able to back into the life you were meant to lead. Knowing how you want the story to end and who will keep your book of life on their bookshelf will help you with each draft and chapter of your journey.

I learned of a wonderful legacy a couple of years ago when my eldest son, Buckley, married Tess, a wonderful young lady from Michigan. Tess and her family belonged to an incredible church called The Kirk In The Hills. The story of how this church came to be moved me so incredibly and is an excellent example to illustrate the importance of creating a legacy.

Kirk in the Hills was the dream and vision of Colonel Edwin S. George, a Detroit businessman whose gift of his home and estate (Cedarholm) in 1947 made Kirk possible. As early as 1933, he saw the need for a church in this area and established the George Foundation for that purpose. The congregation was organized by the Presbytery of Detroit in 1947, and the first services were held that year in Cedarholm Chapel (formerly Colonel George's music room). The cornerstone for the church was laid in 1951, the same year Colonel George died. His remains are entombed under the narthex of the Kirk's sanctuary.

Patterned after Scotland's Melrose Abbey, Kirk in the Hills is a majestic, gothic-style church, located on a 41-acre lakeside setting 20 miles north of Detroit.

Talk about a legacy! If this wonderful man, Colonel Edwin S. George, hadn't gifted this magnificent property, then thousands of lives would not have been influenced and my son and his new bride would not have had this incredible place to begin their lives. You will never know how many people you have touched while here and after you've passed on but it's more than you know and it's worth investing your time into planning to make sure you leave a lasting legacy...parting gifts that are part of you.

To be clear, legacy doesn't have to be as grand as a church and can be as simple as leaving special mementos behind for your family. The objective here is to make sure you've done your due diligence and ensured your parting gifts are part of you. Whether it's setting up a trust, will or estate planning, it's important for you to design your legacy as a continuation of your life well lived and well planned.

Legacy is not purely financial either. Your time and effort investments in your grandchildren, community or charity are all wonderful examples of leaving something intentional behind. Your Future Funnel™ is meant to inspire and motivate you to find the WHY in your life. If you're going through the motions without a WHY, things can seem less meaningful and lack purpose. That is why this book is entitled: The Passion and Purpose Project. It's your time to discover your passion, define your purpose and know your WHY.

YOUR FUTURE FUNNEL™

- DESIRES
- AVERSIONS
- LIFESTYLE
- METRICS
- PREPARATION
- ACTION
- LEGACY

YOUR FUTURE

Chapter 8

My Future Funnel
– What Will You Do?

"Change makes you find your calling, your legacy, and God's divine plan for your life. Don't run from it."

— Iman

In the time I've been working on this book, I have talked to numerous individuals about Your Future Funnel™, and it's been very exciting to hear how many people do want to feel that they are in creative control of their lives. It's like the ultimate DIY project. It can be exciting, fun, and ever changing, just like you.

About one year into working on this, I began to ask myself if I was living and practicing the Your Future Funnel™ concepts. That is, was I taking my own advice? I opened up a conversation with my husband about it, specifically the legacy/retirement idea, since we are now both in our 50's, and I had an incredible revelation. First, I realized I was not completely following my own advice, and, secondly, we gained clarity on how we wanted to "retire."

This was both revelatory and super exciting to me because I realized I needed this advice (which reinforced why I was writing the book) and it opened up a great collaborative moment with my husband, which lead us to the decision to sell our downtown Charleston home and, in exchange, purchase a "forever" home on Fripp Island and a waterfront downtown Charleston condo at a marina. We realized that we want to one day raise our grandchildren and retire on Fripp Island (a small barrier island outside of Beaufort, SC) and also keep a landing pad or pied-à-terre in Charleston for work and fun. While this may change over time, it's a work in progress, and we are designing it together.

We also hired an incredible wealth/legacy planner and he's been working with us to get a plan in place for our long-term goals and legacy planning. I can't begin to tell you how much more focused we are now on reaching these goals because we actually know what we want, can get creative on how to achieve it, and are paying attention in a more strategic way. Again, going back to the car analogy, once you know where you are going, you're going to pay attention to the gauges, find the best way to your destination, and be in control of the steering.

Just like an adventurous road trip, your life excursion can be an exciting journey that you are always navigating. Since opening my second spa downtown Charleston in 2020, I am now about to open my third spa in Franklin, Tennessee, a fourth spa in Savannah, Georgia. I'm also speaking on topics such as hospitality, entrepreneurship, and female empowerment. I have become an angel investor and am learning about new businesses that I'm interested in exploring. I see over and over again how all this is connected to my inner child who wanted to help people become successful, teach, cheer others on, and serve. Taking on the Passion and Purpose Project firsthand, has enabled me to live **MY FUTURE FUNNEL** and continue to embrace change and spot opportunities. Having a good plan gives me the framework and confidence to make bold decisions with more intention.

So, what will you do? Where will you go? What lifestyle will you live? What dreams will you fulfill? Who will you help along the way? Your journey is waiting to unfold. I encourage you to create YOUR FUTURE FUNNEL™ and make it unique, just like you!

One Last Thing before you go...

One of my favorite things to do is paddle board or take a walk on the beach and listen to an episode of the Podcast: *How I Built That* (HIBT). There is one episode in particular that resonated with me and really represents much of what I have tried to convey in this book. It was Bobbi Brown (Bobbi Brown Cosmetics). I won't retell the entire episode here, but I certainly encourage you to take a listen. There were a few key moments in the podcast that had my head nodding and me smiling in agreement. The first is that Bobbi didn't like the college she attended her freshman year and considered dropping out. She had a conversation with her mother, who she idolized, and her mother regretted not completing college herself and asked Bobbi, "What would you do if it were your birthday today and you could do anything you wanted?" Bobbi told her that she would want to go to the department store and try on make-up. Her mother then encouraged her to find a college where she could study make-up and Bobbi did just that.

YFF Lesson here: She knew what she didn't want, she knew what she loved to do (inner child), and she asked for help (winning team/connecting/talking about it).

I absolutely LOVE this and also love that she had a mother who encouraged her to find a new path.

Later in the podcast, she was talking about how she couldn't live within her budget when she was just starting as a make-up artist. Her father told her to quit worrying about the budget and worry about making more money. This is great advice.

YFF Lesson here: Know your numbers. You need to make sure you know how much you're making and then work back into what you can afford to reach your goals. Focus on the goal and again, have a winning team. She went to her father for advice, and he helped her, but oftentimes we are afraid to ask for help.

As her business grew, Bobbi took on partners in order to grow. Although she later admitted that having friends as partners isn't ideal, she couldn't have done it without them. She knew that she didn't understand all aspects of the business to be able to scale and grow it. Toward the end of the podcast, she said that she really wasn't good at anything other than telling those around her what to do, so she made sure to hire the best of the best, especially for the things she knew weren't her areas of expertise.

YFF Lesson here: You don't have to do it all or know it all. You don't have to do it alone. It's okay to take on partners when it makes sense and hire others. It's also very important to hire people that are great at the things you aren't so great at to help the business grow collectively. This isn't the answer for every individual or entrepreneur, but it's important to know that you have options and there is more than one way to skin a cat.

The host of the podcast asked Bobbi near the end of the episode if she regretted selling the company to Estee Lauder. Bobbi said that she absolutely didn't at all and that she knew that she was creative and an entrepreneur and that she wanted to spend time with friends and family. Being a billionaire wasn't as important to her as freedom and autonomy.

YFF Lesson Here: It's YOUR FUTURE... this should be about what you want, not what others think of you or some label, etc. You need to find your passion and purpose as Bobbi did and the rest will work itself out with solid planning, networking, and hard work.

Your future is bright! Don't fear the unknown but take a calculated risk to do what fulfills you, live where you want to live, and enjoy the things that bring you happiness. Find your passion and your purpose! I look forward to seeing you at the top!

ABOUT THE AUTHOR

Kimmy K. Powell

Kimmy K. Powell is a mentor, author, speaker, angel investor and serial entrepreneur with 30+ years of expertise building and scaling multiple 7-figure businesses. Her expertise spans a diverse portfolio of construction to luxury hospitality. Today, Kimmy is a vocal advocate for young, passionate, budding entrepreneurs providing them framework and momentum in their early ventures.

She was born in Dayton, Ohio and graduated from University of Dayton with a B.S. in Computer Science. Her early experience with IBM and Lexis/Nexis helped shape her professional experience and business acumen. In 1991, she joined her husband and founded several companies in Construction and Commercial Real Estate. After relocating to Charleston in 2014, she began a career in hospitality and currently owns two 9,000 sq. ft. luxury spas (Woodhouse Spas, Inc.) in Charleston, South Carolina, a 6,000 sq. ft. location in Franklin, Tennessee and she will be opening the doors to a 6,000 sq. ft. location in Savannah, Georgia in Summer 2023.

She and her husband of 33 years, Keith, have raised three sons who have flourished into ventures of their own. She splits her time between their residences in Downtown Charleston and Fripp Island, S.C. In her free time, she enjoys reading, boating, traveling, mentoring, writing and spending time with friends and family. She lends her time and talents to the Harbour Club Executive Committee Board, The College of Charleston Board of Governors, The American Lung Association and many more community and philanthropic endeavors.

Work with
Kimmy K. Powell

Kimmy K. Powell is passionate about helping others and inspiring you to be your uniquely awesome self. She speaks on many panels and podcasts on topics such as Hospitality, Entrepreneurship, Parenting, Female Business Owners, Investments, and Spa Life.

If you are interested in learning more, contacting, working with, or collaborating with Kimmy, please reach out to her at: info@kimmykpowell or visit **kimmykpowell.com**

Made in the USA
Columbia, SC
29 November 2023

27405684R00080